FLYING FISH
Darla Duhaime

Before & After Reading Activities

Teaching Focus:
Concepts of Print- Have students find capital letters and punctuation in a sentence. Ask students to explain the purpose for using them in a sentence.

Before Reading:

Building Academic Vocabulary and Background Knowledge
Before reading a book, it is important to set the stage for your child or student by using pre-reading strategies. This will help them develop their vocabulary, increase their reading comprehension, and make connections across the curriculum.

1. *Read the title and look at the cover. Let's make predictions about what this book will be about.*
2. *Take a picture walk by talking about the pictures/photographs in the book. Implant the vocabulary as you take the picture walk. Be sure to talk about the text features such as headings, Table of Contents, glossary, bolded words, captions, charts/diagrams, or Index.*
3. *Have students read the first page of text with you then have students read the remaining text.*
4. *Strategy Talk – use to assist students while reading.*
    - *Get your mouth ready*
    - *Look at the picture*
    - *Think…does it make sense*
    - *Think…does it look right*
    - *Think…does it sound right*
    - *Chunk it – by looking for a part you know*
5. *Read it again.*

Content Area Vocabulary
Use glossary words in a sentence.

glide
predators
surface
torpedo

After Reading:

Comprehension and Extension Activity
After reading the book, work on the following questions with your child or students in order to check their level of reading comprehension and content mastery.

1. *How do flying fish glide above the water? (Summarize)*
2. *What do flying fish eat? (Asking Questions)*
3. *Where might you see a flying fish? (Text to Self Connection)*
4. *How do flying fish escape predators? (Asking Questions)*

Extension Activity
Make flying fish spinners! With just some construction paper and scissors, you can make a school of flying fish. For complete instructions, visit *http://onetimethrough.com/how-to-make-fantastic-flying-fish-paper-spinners*.

Table of Contents

Flying Fish	4
Taking Flight	10
Gliding and Swimming	15
Fun Facts	22
Picture Glossary	23
Index	24
Websites to Visit	24
About the Author	24

Flying Fish

Most fish have fins. But flying fish have fins that work like wings on an airplane!

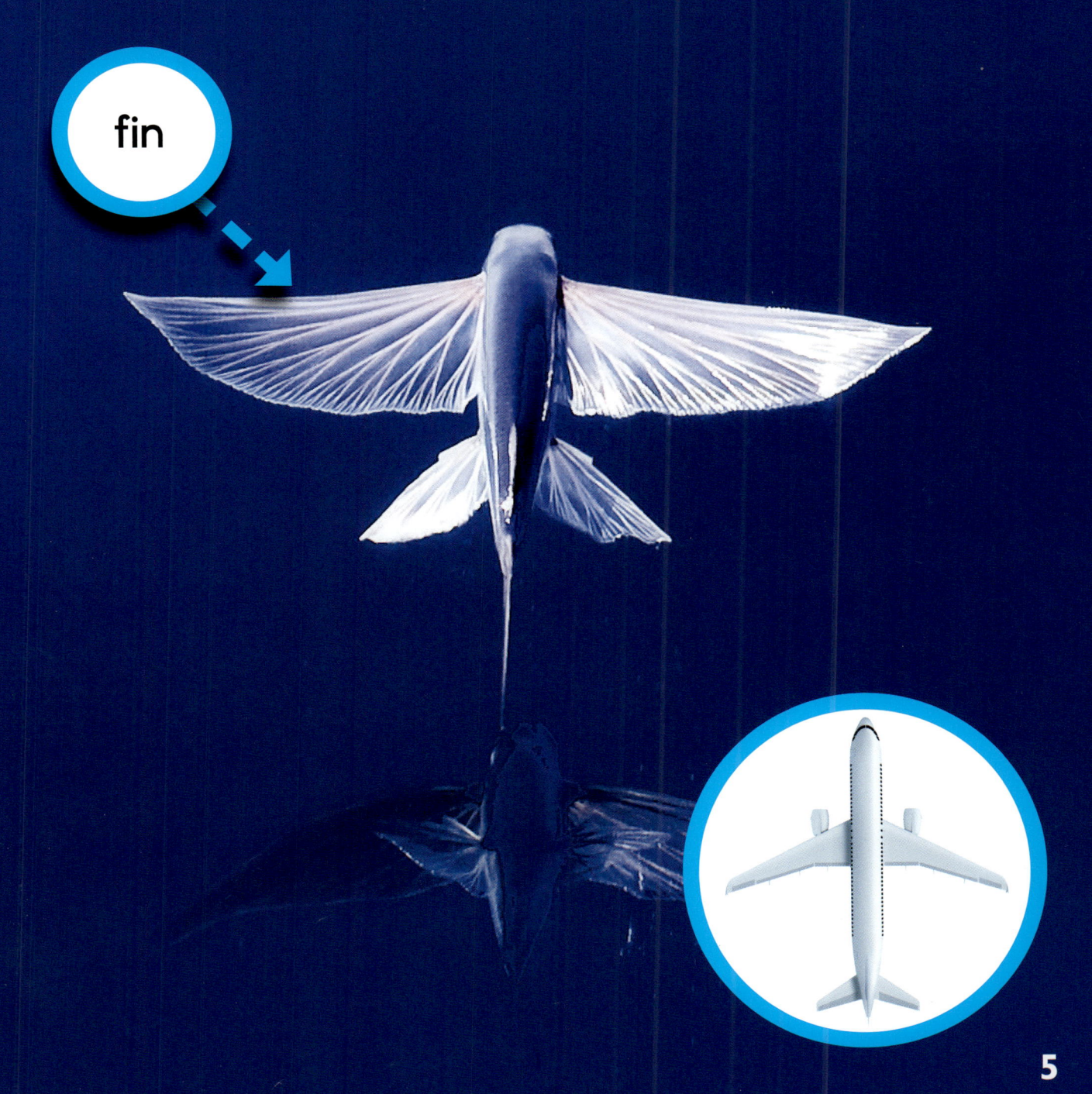

Tuna, marlin, and dolphin like to eat flying fish.

Flying fish **glide** above the water to escape these hungry **predators**.

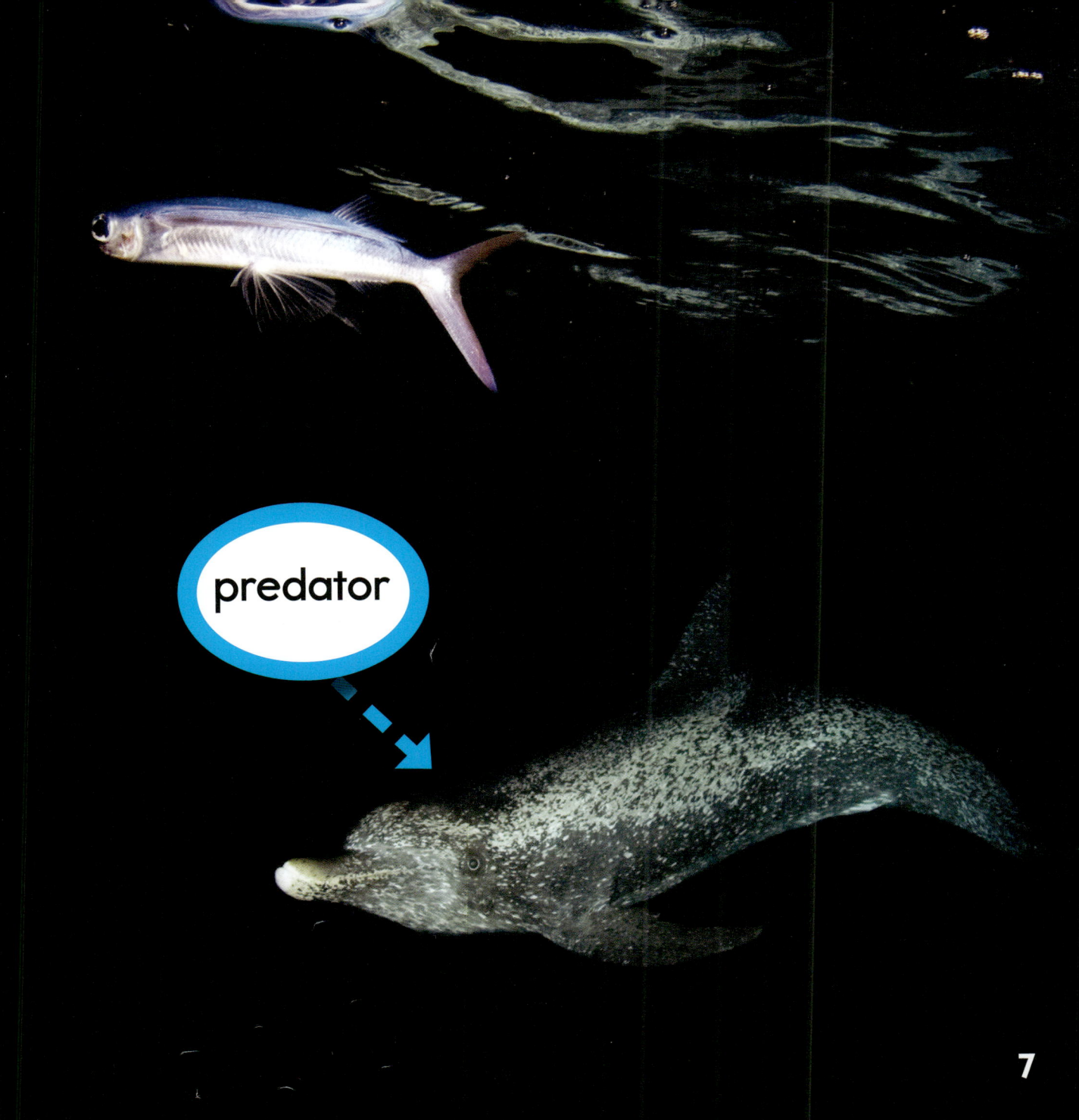

Flying fish travel in schools, or groups. They eat smaller fish and plankton.

plankton

Taking Flight

A flying fish's body is shaped like a **torpedo**. It has a forked tail. The forked tail moves fast! The fish races toward the water's **surface**.

torpedo

The flying fish bursts out of the water. Its pectoral fins extend.

Gliding and Swimming

The air under its fins pushes the fish upward. It takes off like an airplane!

Flying fish can glide for about 650 feet (198 meters) at a time.

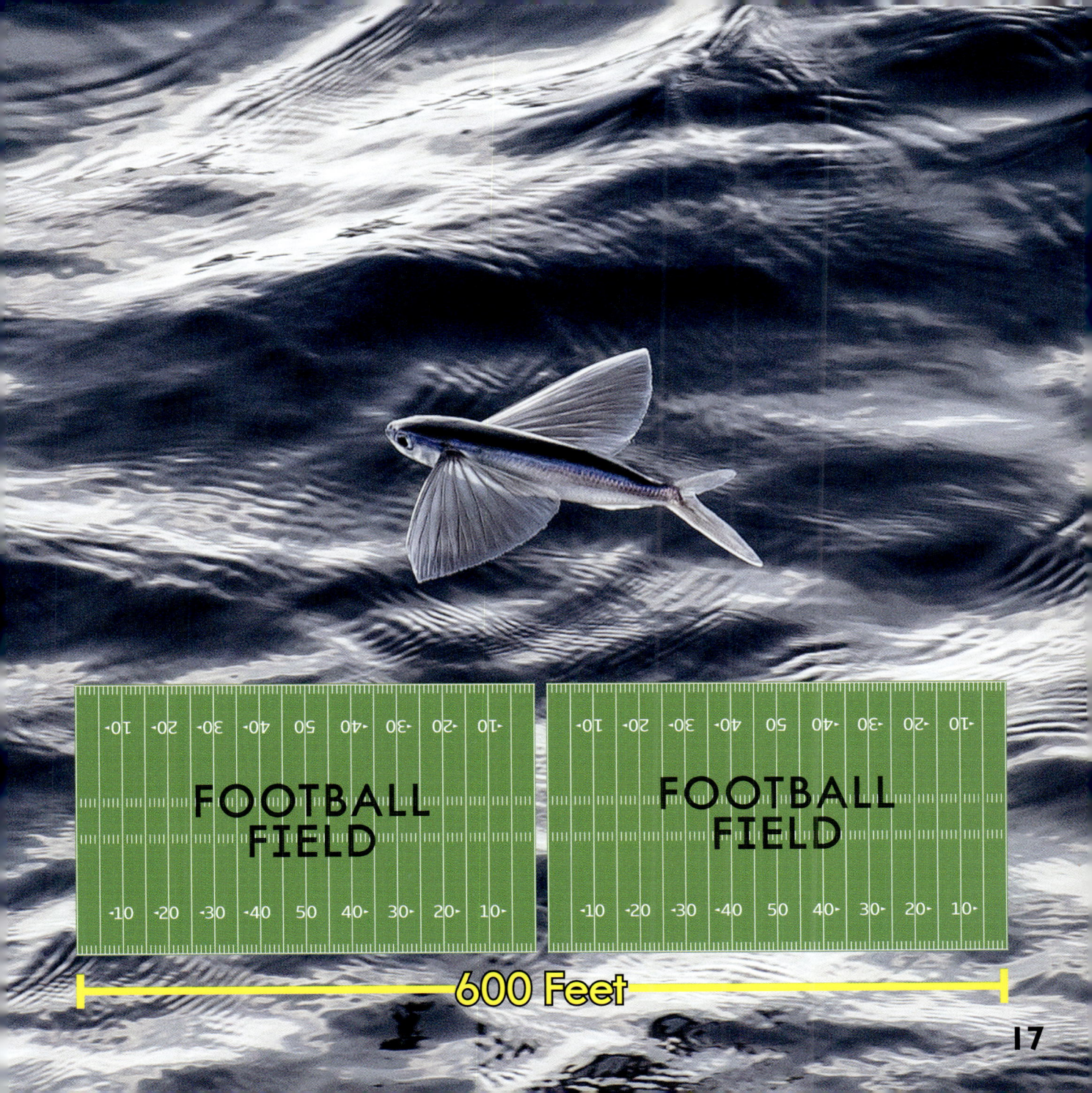

FOOTBALL FIELD FOOTBALL FIELD

600 Feet

A bird flies by flapping its wings. Flying fish cannot flap their pectoral fins. They flap their tails against the water to stay in the air.

Wings are great for flying. But not so great for swimming! Flying fish fold their fins against their sides to swim.

Fun Facts

- There are about 40 species of flying fish. They are found in the open waters of the Atlantic, Pacific, and Indian oceans.

- Flying fish can swim about 37 miles (60 kilometers) per hour.

- They beat their tails about 70 times per second while racing toward the surface.

- Flying fish can soar up to four feet (1.22 meters) above the water.

Picture Glossary

glide (glide): To fly without power, like a glider.

predators (PRED-uh-turs): Animals that hunt other animals for food.

surface (SUR-fis): The outside or outermost layer of something.

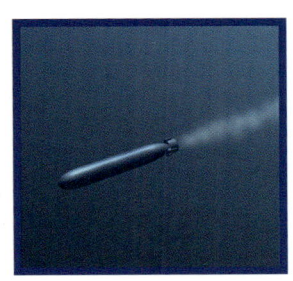
torpedo (tor-PEE-doh): An underwater missile that is shot from a ship or submarine.

Index

fin(s) 4, 5, 12, 13, 15, 18, 20
predator(s) 6, 7
schools 8
swimming 20
tail(s) 10, 18, 19

Websites to Visit

http://animals.nationalgeographic.com/animals/fish/flying-fish
www.softschools.com/facts/animals/flying_fish_facts/318
http://kids.britannica.com/elementary/article-390146/flying-fish

Meet The Author!
www.meetREMauthors.com

About the Author

Darla Duhaime is fascinated by sea creatures and their amazing ocean habitats. When she is not writing books for kids, you can often find her gazing at the ocean, dreaming up new stories.

© 2018 Rourke Educational Media

All rights reserved. No part of this book may be reproduced or utilized in any form or by any means, electronic or mechanical including photocopying, recording, or by any information storage and retrieval system without permission in writing from the publisher.

www.rourkeeducationalmedia.com

PHOTO CREDITS: Cover and title page: ©Daniel Huebner; p.5, 23: ©bartuchna@yahoo.pl; p.5: ©Edi_Eco; p.7, 20-21, 23: ©Nature Picture Library/Alamy Stock Photo; p.8-9: ©WILDLIFE GmbH/Alamy Stock Photo; p.11: ©Andre Seale/Alamy Stock Photo; p.11, 23: ©Snaprender; p13: ©WaterFrame/Alamy Stock Photo; p.14-15: ©B.A.E./Alamy Stock Photo; p.17, 19, 23: ©Anthony Pierce/Alamy Stock Photo

Edited by: Keli Sipperley
Cover and Interior design by: Rhea Magaro-Wallace

Library of Congress PCN Data

Flying Fish / Darla Duhaime
(Ocean Animals)
ISBN (hard cover)(alk. paper) 978-1-68342-326-3
ISBN (soft cover) 978-1-68342-422-2
ISBN (e-Book) 978-1-68342-492-5
Library of Congress Control Number: 2017931173

Printed in the United States of America, North Mankato, Minnesota